Common Sense Recovery:

Dealing with Divorce

Terry Bell & Steve Joiner

ACU Press

Bell, Terry, 1948-
    Common sense recovery: dealing with divorce / Terry
Bell & Steve Joiner.
        p. cm.
    Includes bibliographical references (p.).
    1. Divorce--United States. 2. Children of divorced parents--United
States. 3.Divorce--Religious aspects--Christianity.
I. Joiner, Steve, 1958- . II. Title.
HQ834.B44 1990
306.89--dc20   89-29010
                                                         CIP

Typesetting and Cover Design, Mel Ristau/Design
Illustration, Mel Ristau
Printed in the United States of America

ISBN 0-89112-094-7, Paper

5 4 3 2 1

Dedication

TERRY BELL

TO JAN, MY WIFE AND BEST FRIEND, AND OUR CHILDREN, BETHANY AND MARSHALL, WHOM I ADORE.

STEVE JOINER

TO MY WIFE LINDA, FOR LOVING AND SUPPORTING ME WHEN I WAS TOO BUSY.

TO MY BOYS, CRAIG AND BRYAN, FOR SHARING THEIR DADDY WITH SO MANY OTHERS.

Contents

Common Sense Recovery:

Dealing with Divorce

Terry Bell & Steve Joiner

Redeeming the Second Best

What do you do when life hands you a major disappointment? In the beginning, you had wanted this marriage to work. Perhaps you still do. Divorce was not what you had planned or wanted. You had always dreamed that your marriage would be the best. So what do you do when life hands you something less than the best?

The biblical record is filled with examples of good people who had to face big disappointments. Genesis 21:8-19 provides us with just such an account. Here we discover Abraham learning to deal with disappointment. Remember Abraham? The father of the faithful! An honoree in God's Hall of Fame! Next to Christ, he was perhaps the most influential man in history. Three world religions (Moslems, Jews, and Christians) trace their beginnings back to him. Nevertheless he was human with faults and disappointments just like you and me.

The story of Abraham's disappointment begins to unfold in Genesis 15 where we read of God's promise that he would be the father of a great nation. Years went by and there was no sign of the realization of this promise. Abraham and Sarah remained childless. In an effort to try to help God, the two of them concocted a scheme by which the aging Abraham might have a child. He slept with one of his maid-servants, she conceived, and Ishmael was born. But, to Abraham's surprise, God didn't need any help. God's train was running right on schedule. A short time later, by the will of God, Isaac, the child of promise, was born to Abraham and Sarah.

Abraham had his hands full. Sarah had developed a hatred for Ishmael and his mother, Hagar. As the boys grew, Sarah's contempt for Ishmael and Hagar grew. The boys didn't get along, (their descendants, the Arabs and the Jews, still don't!) How do you deal with an "Ishmael" when you had wanted an "Isaac"? How do you deal with a broken marriage when you wanted yours to be the best?

From time to time we all get stuck with something that we had not wanted and had not planned. Everyone in some areas has to come to grips with second best. You wanted this marriage to work. When you said the vows, you meant them. You wanted your marriage to be symbolically like an "Isaac," the fulfillment of happiness ever after. Instead you have ended up with an "Ishmael," a disappointment now out of your control, yet something you started with high hopes. What do you do?

Perhaps the first thing to understand is what NOT to do. Sarah is the best example for this. The few word pictures of Sarah that surface from the biblical account of this period of her life give us a glimpse of a spiritually sick, emotionally unhealthy woman. She is being controlled by her prejudices and her wounded ego. (One definition of an emotional illness is that you don't mind, in fact you enjoy, seeing other people hurt.)

It was desperation that got her into this problem in the first place. She was the one who suggested that Abraham unite with Hagar and produce Ishmael (Gen. 16:1-2). Here is a woman who was driven to the point of neurosis because she could not settle into God's schedule. Then, when Ishmael finally was born, she resorts to the defense mechanisms of denial, escape, and compensation (in this case, arrogance.) The worst way to handle an "Ishmael" is to pretend it never happened.

The Old Testament picture of Sarah at this time in her life is a picture of all the wrong ways to handle an Ishmael. She goes beyond the travesty of refusing to own up to her mistakes; she actually has the audacity to try to blame it on someone else–Hagar. That's sick...neurotic. How can we ever hope to gain any redemptive power in our lives as long as we are trying to escape the realities of "second best." We could all find a "Hagar" to blame it on, and many of us do.

Speaking of "Hagar," we find another example of how not to handle disappointment. She was a victim and she would have let you know it. Allowing hatred to come into her heart (Genesis 16:4), she became consumed with self-pity and arrogance. Her arrogance compensated for her inadequate self-image. Her self-pity promoted her self-perception that she would always be a victim of circumstance. She played the martyr well and, in doing so, nurtured the very characteristics that made her emotionally unstable. In my counseling, I have seen many "Hagars."

As we read this biblical account of how to handle disappointments, we sense a developing maturity in

Abraham. Between chapters 16 and 21, he grew up emotionally. Ishmael was also his son. He did not seek to escape from that fact nor did he seek to deny it. He was now faced with a situation of "damage control." He had to face one of life's second bests. He dealt with it by listening very carefully to God.

It was at this point that God's redemptive action went to work. Genesis 21:17 says, "God heard the voice of the boy." The name Ishmael means "God Hears." God hears the cries of our disappointments. He hears the pain of our second bests. It is in the midst of that disappointment and pain that God begins his redemptive ministry. And God rescued Ishmael.

Redeeming second best situations is perhaps the finest expression of God's love. He saved us while we were yet disappointments to Him. Jesus came to a second best world, a world which had become a disappointment. He came not just to condemn it, but to redeem it. We have all had an "Ishmael" in our lives at one time or another. Then God begins to work.

It is not the authors' plan in this book to minimize divorce. Divorce is always a tragedy, a disappointment, an Ishmael. The Bible is very clear: God hates divorce. No one understands that better right now than you. The road to complete recovery is long and difficult. But it is not impossible. *God is still able to redeem our second best!*

Chapter 1

Where Do "I" Go from Here?

Anything is Survivable IF...

It was almost unbelievable! I was actually sitting in the home of Professor Victor Frankl. I had admired him for years, read much of his work, and patterned much of my own counseling after some of the principles he had demonstrated. And now to have this private audience with him was a time I'll never forget. At the end of our visit, he showed me a picture hanging on his study wall of an old German barracks. The front courtyard was strewn with recyclable caskets. With obvious emotion, Dr. Frankl pointed to the building and said, "It was in this building that my mother gave me her final blessing. She put her hands on my shoulders and said words to me that I shall never forget. The next day she was transferred to Auschwitz. Within a week she was herded into the gas chambers. I never saw her again."

And then pointing to the caskets in the foreground of the picture, Professor Frankl said, "I was on casket duty. Our job was to take the bodies of dead prisoners and transport them in the caskets to the mass graves and then return with the caskets for more bodies. On one of the trips, I looked down into a casket and to my horror, I saw the corpse of my father." Tears were coming into his eyes as he recalled the tragic events. I asked, "Herr Professor Doctor, how does one survive such horror?" He looked straight into my eyes and said, "My friend, anything is survivable if one has reason to survive." Those words are indelibly printed on my heart.

"Anything is survivable!" Of course there are physical limits to this, but are there actually limits to what the emotions can survive? Every person who is experiencing divorce will no doubt ask this question over and over. "Will I make it? Will I survive?"

What is your reason for surviving? What is your reason for going on with life? Maybe it's your family. Maybe it's your faith. Maybe it's your career or something else. A person simply has to have a reason for going on. To be obsessed with the past is to waste the present and the future. Those who make it through the recovery period best are those who find reason to pursue the future. The apostle Paul said, "But one thing I do: Forgetting what is behind and straining toward what is ahead, I press on...(Philippians 3:13-14).

Divorce recovery is a journey. There has to be something you are looking forward to at the end of the trip. Ultimately it is the eternal principles that make life worth living. A personal relationship with the Lord can give meaning to the most difficult of circumstances.

Just another stage

One of the most comforting thoughts to parents of young children is that whatever bad behavior their child is currently involved in, hopefully, it's just another stage that will soon pass. The "terrible twos" don't last forever.

That's the way it is with recovering from divorce. Whether you look at these time phases as stages, building blocks, stair steps, or whatever, there is a journey to be taken and it is taken step by step, stage by stage.

For a number of years, therapists have been attempting to describe the path to divorce recovery by listing the various stages one goes through as the trip is made. It is helpful to notice some of the lists that have been compiled. Your journey may take some different side roads, but usually the same basic direction is traveled by all. Here are several prominent lists of stages:

Basic Stages of Divorce

Bohannan	*Kessler*	*Froiland & Hozman*
1971	*1975*	*1977*
Emotional divorce	Disillusionment	Denial
Legal divorce	Erosion	Anger
Economic divorce	Detachment	Bargaining
Co-parent divorce	Physical Separation	Depression
Community divorce	Mourning	Acceptance
Psychic divorce	Second Adolescence	Hard Work

One of the most definitive lists of stages in recent years has been compiled by Bruce Fisher. He has observed that the journey to recovery involves Denial, Loneliness, Guilt/Rejection, Grief, Anger, Letting Go, Self-concept, Friendship, Leftovers, Love, Trust, Sexuality, Responsibility, Singleness, and finally Freedom. For one who is experiencing the pain of divorce, it should be helpful to know that there is a light at the end of the tunnel.

It is not our purpose in this book to examine each one of the stages in detail. Basically we want to give a general overview of the process of recovery. A basic understanding of the journey, however, should help you to know if you're still on the right track and help you gauge the distance to your final destination of complete recovery. Stage by stage, step by step, the road to recovery must be traveled. For those who are traveling with children, the journey is all the more difficult. At a time when children are in need of the highest quality of parenting, the parents are least able to provide it. How do you help someone else who is hurting when you're hurting so badly yourself? There are things you can do. Even though children will suffer emotional pain, they are amazingly resilient. With the children it is not a question of sheltering them from the agony, rather it becomes a matter of providing them with the resources necessary to cope with the change.

FOR THE KIDS

Birds have it so much better than humans. They are beautifully awesome as they freely soar above the earth. I want to fly, not in a plane, but like a bird sailing over the valleys, farmlands, and cities. But it would be silly, not to mention dangerous, for me to climb to the top of the nearest high rise and jump, flapping my arms, in hopes of joining the birds. Soon after the jump, this bird lover would be kissing concrete. Why? You can't fight the natural laws of gravity. You take the jump; you suffer the consequences.

The same holds true for children of divorced families. The parents have taken the jump. The children suffer the fall. Parents cannot, and perhaps should not, protect them from the fall.

Did you say "Don't protect my child?"

As much as parents hate to admit it, the child will suffer for the decisions of the parents. They will not be able to circumvent the pain and confusion of the family breakup. The child must deal with the stages of grief and special struggles that accompany this disorienting experience. Any attempt to hide the child from the painful process will only prolong the difficult recovery process.

What can I do?

Simply, and painfully, accept the fact that the divorce will cause trauma for your children. Understand the special struggles that children endure during this process and affirm your love for them. Children of divorced families suffer through many of the same stages that have been outlined earlier in this chapter. In most cases, they also suffer other significant trauma associated with the divorce. Let's talk about this special pain.

"Everyone I care about leaves me!"

For every child, the breakup causes an intense sense of loss. The family security that they have always trusted dies. The natural reaction of the child is to resist loving anyone else. A ten-year-old boy may give up on his dream of owning a dog and, when pushed for a reason for this sudden change, he screams, "Why own a dog? He will just run away and leave me, too!"

Even though you, as the custodial parent, know that you will not leave, the child does not. Be patient and understand that this loss is inherently different from yours. It is an extremely complex loss and will require time for the child to adjust to the new environment.

"If only I bad been a better kid!"

The most insidious effect of the whole divorce process is the tendency of the children to blame themselves for the split. They assume that past bad behavior put stress on Mom and Dad. This stress, in turn, contributed to the breakup.

One father spoke of receiving a letter from his seven-year-old daughter that read, "Daddy, I promise to mind and be a good girl if you will come home."

Parents need to follow two simple rules in trying to help their children deal with these guilty feelings.

1. Do not allow the child to take any blame for the breakup. The parents chose to marry and at least one chose to leave.

2. Do not intensify these feelings of guilt by making the child choose sides in the divorce. They already will tend to have strong negative feelings toward one of the parents. Don't encourage these feelings.

"Someday Mom and Dad will get back together!"

Many children fantasize that the parents will reconcile their differences. They may harbor dreams of returning to happier days. This fantasy is one of the reasons that some children resist a second marriage. The new relationship will only make the fulfillment of those dreams more difficult. With some children, these dreams never die.

She was twenty-five years old. Her parents had been divorced for over ten years. Both had remarried and had established separate lives. Yet she stated, "I think that someday Mom and Dad will get back together."

A parent should avoid extremes. Neither encourage nor ridicule the dream. Even if reconciliation is a possibility, do not add extra stress to the child by feeding the fantasy. Remember, this stage is normal and even necessary for some children to accept the reality of a separated family.

Hope lies in the future

I love old movies, especially Tarzan movies. The jungle man and his animal friends remind me of lazy Saturday afternoons at the theater. Yet, one scene was a staple of every Tarzan movie. The natives would capture someone and sentence him to death. They would pull two sapling trees to the ground and tie the victim's wrists to each tree. Then, to my horror, the ropes were cut and the poor soul met a grisly death.

Unfortunately, those in divorced families who do not deal adequately with these stages of separation may suffer a similar fate of being pulled apart emotionally. The pain of the divorce causes some people to live in the past, to rehash old wounds, or to fantasize about reuniting the family. But hope and recovery lie in the future. Let go of the past and be propelled toward a productive life with your children. Your children will recover as you recover.

Chapter 2

I Feel Guilty;
I Feel Rejected

The road to recovery begins differently in most cases for the two divorced partners. At least one therapist has coined a description for each partner which, though insensitive in some ways, certainly pinpoints the feelings you may have toward yourself at this stage of the process. There are, says Bruce Fisher, the "Dumpers" and the "Dumpees." The Dumper begins this road by having to deal with guilt; the Dumpee, rejection. Both paths are rocky, it's just that there are different rocks, chuck holes, and detours on this temporary fork in the road.

Now you may be one of the lucky few who belong to a third group, which is much more rare than the Dumpers or the Dumpees, but nevertheless in existence. This group Fisher calls the "Mutuals." The Mutuals are those fortunate couples that somehow manage to stay friends. How this happens, nobody knows for sure; but when it does happen, it's a lot easier for everyone concerned.

I feel so guilty

The Dumper has a hard row to hoe. If you're the Dumper and you're feeling guilty, you know exactly what I mean. "Look what I've done to my spouse!" "Look what I've done to my children!" "Look what I've done to my parents and in-laws!" These are only a few of the "Look what I've dones." The list, of course, can be as endless as the people who seem to want to add to it.

Here are a few caution signs for the one who is traveling down this particular path.

CAUTION: DON'T SHIFT THE BLAME!

This doesn't mean that you necessarily have to accept ALL the blame either. In my counseling experience I've seen very few, if any, cases where there was just one "guilty party." But there are no good shortcuts on this part of the recovery road. One good thing about feeling guilty is that it proves that you are still human (which you may need reassurance of at this point in the process). Accepting your portion of the blame is a sign that the true healing process is beginning. Jesus always required a simple acknowledgement of wrongdoing before he would bestow the blessings of forgiveness. "If we claim to be without sin, we deceive ourselves and the truth is not in us. If we confess our sins, he is faithful and just and will forgive us our sins and purify us from all unrighteousness" (I John 1:8-9).

Being objective is so difficult. Guilt is such a personal and painful thing that extreme care must be taken not to rationalize beyond reality.

CAUTION: DON'T ENGAGE IN COVER-UP!

The reality is, "In some ways, I blew it." Maybe it was my original decision to marry this person. Maybe it was my inability to communicate my feelings adequately when I first began to feel like the relationship was headed downhill. Maybe... Maybe...Maybe! The possibilities here are endless. Deal with the guilt. Put it behind you.

CAUTION: DON'T BE OBSESSED WITH THE PAST!

"Each day has enough trouble of its own" (Matthew 6:34). While the past certainly needs to be dealt with, what is needed most now is a determination regarding the future. You may have a tendency to ruminate over the past. Whatever amends you need to make, do it now. Set your life straight with as many people as you possibly can. Ask them for forgiveness. Ask God for forgiveness. Whatever apologies you need to make, make them quickly. Repair the splintered edges of your life. Put it behind you and move on. Get on with your life and let the Lord forgive you. Take the words of Jesus seriously, "Go now and leave your life of sin" (John 8:11). Whether you feel like your actions were actually "sin" or not, one thing you must admit is you missed it somewhere along the line. This is probably true for both you and your partner. Basically that's the definition of sin: "missing it." Deal with the past as much as you can and then point yourself toward the future.

But I feel rejected

But what if you're the Dumpee? While you may also have some feelings of guilt, your overwhelming feeling may well be that of rejection. Rejection can leave you so wounded and caught up in self-pity that you may actually begin closing out the rest of the world.

Of course there are certain daily activities that must go on. Children, jobs, housework, shopping, driving, banking, paying the bills, all of this and much more require an enormous amount of energy. Strong feelings of rejection can impair your work in every other aspect of your life.

Rejection injures your sense of self-worth. When your spouse leaves you, the message you get is, "I must not be what I used to be. I have lost the worth that I used to have. My life is so dismal that no one would want to waste their life by spending it with me." Jim Smoke has said, "One of the keys of stabilizing your life is feeling good again about yourself. It is knowing who you are and liking it. It is gaining control from the chaos and establishing priorities and goals...It is walking on the edge without fear of falling off."

The road to recovery really begins to get rocky as it progresses. There are numerous hazards in this portion of the journey. Obeying the caution signs is an absolute must.

CAUTION: DON'T GENERALIZE!

While it may be tempting to engage in a pity party and begin to believe that you have nothing to offer anybody ever again, it's simply not true. Let's face it, we've all got our faults, but we've also got our strengths. Because we've experienced rejection in one relationship does not mean that we will never be able to experience a fulfilling relationship again.

CAUTION: DON'T DISASTERIZE!

Some people, especially after a traumatic occurence like divorce, tend to see a new disaster in every new opportunity. Children are great at disasterizing. "Why should I get a new toy? It'll just break, too!" One counselee said to me, "I hate all men" (generalizing); "all they want to do is just break your heart and then throw you away" (disasterizing).

CAUTION: DON'T WALLOW!

Wallowing in self-pity may make you feel a little better for the time being, but it will also make you sick if you keep it up.

CAUTION: BEWARE OF THE PYGMALION!

This is the trap of the negative self-fufilling prophecy. We tend to act like what we think we are. If I think I'm worthless, I may start acting that way. The more I act that way, the more people tend to avoid me. The more people avoid me, the more I feel rejected. The more I feel rejected the more I feel worthless. It's a vicious cycle that simply must be broken.

CAUTION: BEWARE OF QUICK RELIEF!

Fast relief may be great when you are talking about stomach medicine, but in the area of divorce recovery, it usually spells problems. One temptation is to try to find anything or anyone to fill the vacancy in your life as quickly as possible. This is not a time for big decisions.

FOR THE KIDS

The trauma of divorce is second only to the death of a loved one. Divorce represents separation from security and a loss of control. "Control" is an important issue with children of divorce. Earlier in this chapter, the divorcing parents were classed in the categories of "Dumpers and Dumpees." Children are always the Dumpees in the breakup. In this position, children feel a distressing loss of control in their lives. And with this loss comes feelings of guilt and rejection.

Guilt

Children will many times feel responsible for the breakup of the parents. They do not understand the process of the split and somehow perceive that their behavior was a contributing factor to the breakup. In young children, the child perceives Mom and Dad as almost god-like. They can do nothing wrong. Therefore, if the parents split up, the divorce must be the child's fault.

Even if he understands that his parents are not perfect, the split can be devastating to his self-perception and the child may want to deny the finality of the divorce. Therefore, the child will blame the divorce on himself in an attempt to take control of the situation. If it was his fault, perhaps he can restore the relationship by becoming a better son. In other words, the child feels his vulnerability and loss of control.

Suggestions for dealing with a child's guilty feelings:

1. Encourage one-on-one relationships between your child and other positive role models. Both the custodial and absent parent should make time to reinforce their own positive feelings toward the child. Also, ask other Christian people, such as youth workers or a Sunday school teacher, to find time to reinforce the worth of your child.

2. Consistently communicate that the divorce was not the child's fault. While your child may not be openly struggling with this issue, do not assume that he has bypassed this stage. Sometimes, these feelings are buried deeply in the soul. You may have to patiently communicate circumstances surrounding the divorce over and over before the child accepts his innocence.

3. Let the kid have a bad day. Don't expect him to deal well with his feelings all of the time. Some days are better than others for you and the same is true for your child.

4. Show lots of physical affection. Hugs, kisses, appropriate touching will communicate that your child is still a special part of your life.

Rejection

Many times, children experience intense feelings of rejection from the parent who moved out. Just like the guilt issue, they do not understand the dynamics of the divorce and, therefore, think that the parent doesn't want or love them anymore. The child avoids the absent parent or even dreams about terrible things happening to that person. One young man told of praying that his Dad would die before the next visitation weekend. The boy was reciprocating his feelings of rejection toward his father.

Suggestions for dealing with rejection:

1. Use every opportunity to encourage your child during this time of loss and disappointment.

2. Honestly answer questions that your child has about the divorce without unduly blaming the absent parent. Most parents still love their children very much, no matter how badly the marriage turned out. Communicate that love to the child. However, if the absent parent is the rare one who does not care about the youngster, the custodial parent should not paint a false portrait of the other. Be honest while gently affirming that the divorce was not the child's fault.

Did Dad want to hurt me?

At some point, the custodial parent will need to directly address the issue of rejection. The pain inflicted by divorce can be either unintentional or intentional. Perhaps, you can sit down with your child and describe it the following way.

"Two best friends were playing one day, riding bicycles on a beautiful summer afternoon. While they were playing, one friend was not paying attention and ran into the other. The child on the second bike fell down, scraped her knee, and hurt herself. The first friend felt terrible. But even though he didn't mean to make her fall, the little girl was still hurt.

"Later that day, a third friend joined the two to play. The boy began to pay more attention to the new friend than the old one which made the little girl jealous. She was so angry that she kicked the boy and went home. The little boy hurt very much and she meant for it to hurt.

"When your (Mom or Dad) left, it was like the first story. He did not mean to hurt, but he did. The pain is still there and it will last for a while. But realize, he still loves you very much and does not want to see you hurting."

Some variation of this story may help aid the healing process by helping younger children begin to understand the motivation of a parent who leaves.

Children who are Dumpees and experience rejection must be given time and the proper support to work through their feelings. If that rejection is not resolved, it can carry into adulthood, sabotaging future meaningful relationships.

Chapter 3

Overcoming Anger

Anger is one emotion most of us know something about, from personal experience if nothing else. It is such a powerful emotion that it has led at least one eminent American psychiatrist to announce that it is the "greatest single problem in life." At this stage in your road to recovery, you may know this better than most people.

In fact, when it comes to divorce anger, the word "anger" is almost too peaceful a term. A more appropriate word would probably be "RAGE." Sometimes things even get violent. Often the violence is turned inward and psychosomatic conditions begin to occur. Headaches, ulcers, body tension, and various nervous disorders are only a few of the weapons that cause us to self-destruct. So deadly is this possibility that Minirth and Meier in their book *HAPPINESS IS A CHOICE* wrote, "Pent-up anger is probably the leading cause of death." Anger does for the body what sand would do in the gas tank of your automobile. It clogs up everything.

But then think of all the new problems you are confronting in such a short period of time. Your routine has changed. Now you have to do all the dishes, keep the car gassed up, wash the linens, mow the lawn, and pay the bills. Also your role has changed. You are once again single. People look at you differently. Some want to get to know you better while others may see you bearing the mark of Cain, whatever that was. In the transition period, when life gets out of control, anger is a normal reaction. This is a natural stage in the recovery process that must be experienced. Your successful passage through this treacherous section of the road is essential for complete success to occur in future stages which you will encounter.

Anger resolution

At this point you may be inclined to slam this book shut and announce that you don't ever want to quit being angry at your sorry, no good ex. Well, get hold of your emotions and force yourself to realize that your anger will hurt you more than it will hurt anyone else. On the Polish frontier, there is a statue of a woman who is looking toward Poland with a brooding expression of sadness and loss. The inscription at the base of the statue reads: "Never forget Germans, of what blind hatred has robbed you." Underneath that sentence is a list of the towns which once belonged to Germany and now belong to Poland. Bitterness, anger, and malice tend to hurt us more than anyone else.

Is anger a sin?
Not necessarily! Jesus was certainly angry when he cleansed the Jewish Temple. The admonition of Paul was

"In your anger do not sin" (Ephesians 4:26). An inspired proverb made it clear: "A wise man controls his temper. He knows that anger causes mistakes" (Proverbs 14:29, TLB). Your anger is normal. But now you must direct yourself toward resolving it. Here are some constructive steps you can take toward resolution.

Don't be afraid of your anger.
It proves you are human. Anger is normal, especially during the aftermath of something as traumatic as divorce.

Listen to the way you communicate.
You are responsible for your feelings, thoughts, words, and actions. No one can make you feel, think, say, or do anything. It is inappropriate to say: "You make me so angry." No one can make you angry. More appropriate would be the statement: "I get so angry when you _____." Make your source of control internal rather than external. The Christian who has the advantage of the indwelling Holy Spirit certainly needs to appropriate this blessing at this point of learning to deal with anger.

Make it a point to be in control when communicating with your ex.
Keep telling yourself to be relaxed and calm. Do not let your former partner's actions or words cause you to lose your control. You don't have to say everything you're thinking. It is, of course, important to express your feelings, but learn to do that in ways that don't escalate the tension. Remember your words are not only a result of your feelings but they are also a means of intensifying feeling. In the New Testament, James said, "When we put bits into the mouths of horses to make

them obey us, we can turn the whole animal...or take ships as an example. Although they are so large and are driven by strong winds, they are steered by a very small rudder wherever the pilot wants to go. Likewise the tongue is a small part of the body, but it makes great boasts" (James 3:3-5). In other words, your words will help heal your thoughts or they will hurt you and prolong the pain. It's up to you. Also, be sure to listen to what is being said to you. Work on being comfortable with communicating with your ex.

Outgrow the need for revenge.
You need to get beyond the point hoping that he/she is feeling as much pain as you are. True, these are difficult barriers to hurdle and it will take a great deal of emotional energy and effort but remember your goal is personal recovery. Grow beyond the need to try to get people on your side. This is a difficult stage to endure. Be patient with yourself and others. Anger in the beginning is normal, but for successful recovery, you've got to get through it. Expect the pain, but remember it is not always going to be like this.

Perhaps the greatest temptation for the one who has been rejected is to engage in a behavior that we will call "martyring." It is a condition which tries to make others believe that all of the current suffering has been inflicted on you by the other. "Look what you've done to me. It's all your fault that I'm having to live in this awful apartment. It's all your fault that I've got the flu. It's all your fault that I've lost my job."

Martyring is a behavioral mechanism used to trigger guilt. It is really a subtle attempt at revenge. Some of the charges may even be true. Maybe you are hating your apartment, your new job, maybe to some extent all of that is a result of decisions made by your former spouse. So what good does it do to dwell on all that now?

A sign of growth will be your ability to start trying to heal the wounds between you and your ex. This doesn't mean that this can be done in every case. No doubt there are cases where healing will be impossible. But don't you be the one who makes it impossible. The goal here should not be reconciliation. It some cases that may happen and remarriage occur, but now that the divorce has been granted, the likelihood of that happening is probably pretty slim. Your goal should not even be to reestablish friendship. Your goal is recovery. The quicker you can overcome the anger and let the hurts heal, the quicker you can get on with life.

FOR THE KIDS

"It was late December when Mom moved out. It was like the grinch who stole Christmas. Everything that was warm and fuzzy went with her...I hated her for that."

Anger is a natural result for children who feel abandoned by a parent. This person, whom they trusted completely, is gone, leaving them angrily resenting this disruption in their lives. In most cases, the children understand only that someone has left them and do not grasp the complexity of the breakup. Therefore, they will at times have a tendency to blame everything on one parent.

A vicious cycle

Children deal with the anger in different ways. Some internalize the rage and do not reveal their struggles to others. Some parents encourage this hiding of emotions. It is very easy for a parent not to allow the child to be angry. They think that by ignoring the problem, it will go away. Unfortunately, when a child suppresses his anger, it may explode on the scene later. Some minor incident will trigger an eruption of pain. One normally quiet 15-year-old boy from a recently divorced family flew into a rage and punched a hole in the living room wall when his mother asked him what time he was coming home that night.

Other children become obviously upset immediately upon the parent's departure. Many custodial parents are uncomfortable with this newly erupted anger and even punish the children for it. One mother was so concerned about her son's sudden outburst of fury that she sent him to his room "until he could get over it!" From the time the other parent leaves, the custodial parent needs to be aware of this "anger potential" in their children. One should realize that changes in behavior may signal underlying struggles with frustration and anger.

This anger is a part of a vicious cycle. He feels guilty that his parents have split up. This guilt becomes frustration over the lack of control in his life and this frustration manifests itself in anger. When parents punish him for his angry outbursts, it produces guilt and the cycle begins again.

Helping my child cope with anger

Feelings are okay. Anger is an emotion and it is natural to experience these emotions during this difficult period of adjustment. A child is not abnormal or bad for feeling angry. In fact, this struggle can even be useful if it spurs that child to do something productive about her situation.

Remember, however, that actions and words are not feelings. It is good to give a child permission to feel angry, but it is not okay to allow that child to be vicious or rude to one of the parents. The parents must teach the child to express pain in a polite way.

No one makes you angry. If possible, communicate to the child that she should not blame her feelings on someone else. She chose to be angry and, at the appropriate time, can choose not to be angry. Teach the child to describe her feelings in terms of herself: "I feel angry" not "you make me mad." The best way to teach the child control is for the parent to model it. Do not expect the youngster to exhibit the proper attitude if Mom gets uncontrollably upset every time Dad calls.

Provide a substitute. Children become angry because something important has been taken away from them (a parent, security, family, etc.). One way to help them recover is to offer substitutions for the loss. New friends or new challenges might be the alternatives that help the child to focus on a fresh beginning.

The parents should form a team. Under no circumstances, no matter how bitter the divorce, should one parent use the children as weapons against the other spouse. The custodial parent may feel that she has found an ally in the child who is also angry with the absent parent. But this attitude is ultimately destructive to everyone.

The parents should form an alliance with each other to aid the recovery of their children. They must put their differences aside long enough to formulate a plan for the healing of their young ones.

When President Ronald Reagan was shot in an assassination attempt, he was delivered to a nearby hospital for surgery to remove the bullet that lay only one inch from his aorta. As he was rolled into surgery, the President said to the medical team, "I hope that all of you are Republicans." One surgeon, who was a liberal Democrat, said, "Today, Mr. President, we are all Republicans." At that critical moment, politics were put aside and they formed a team. Parents should form a similar alliance; the emotional health of your children requires this same kind of commitment. In this one critical area, put aside the politics and pain of the divorce to save your children.

Don't let anger keep you (or your children) from moving toward the future that God has for you. In his book, *Rebuilding*, Bruce Fisher states that his research indicates that the average person stayed angry at their ex-spouse for an average of three years. Allow yourself and your children time to deal with the anger. At the same time, look to the future. Do not use anger as an emotional crutch. Let the fury burn itself out so that you will be free to move on.

Chapter 4

What About
Sexual Intimacy?

Just as one stage of emotional trauma begins to mend, a new challenge presents itself. The absence of sexual intimacy may not be as painful during the times of anger, guilt, and rejection, but there comes a time when these wounds begin to heal and the strong desire for a sexual relationship appears. How does a person deal with this? More specifically, how does a Christian who is committed to a lifestyle of purity manage these strong feelings?

Remember, it was God Himself who said that it is not good for a man (and may I add, a woman) to live alone. It is true that some people can manage this better than others. It may be that you are one of those people who are specially gifted to be single (see I Cor. 7:7). If you are, then you are fortunate indeed, so don't allow anyone to push you into another marriage. It is as uncomfortable for a married person who wants to be single to be married as it is for a single person who wants to be married to stay single. That statement may sound rather confusing but if you think about it a minute I'm sure you'll recognize its truth. For the formerly married, this is a very difficult time indeed. You must not enter this stage unprepared. Here are some things that you can do to help yourself through this trying time:

First, you need to recognize that these feelings are quite natural and in fact, God given. Historically, the early church fathers (and later many of the Christian reformers) brought a great deal of unnecessary baggage into their Christian teaching. Much of their unbiblical doctrine of human sexuality was more a product of the thinking of their time than it was a true exposition of the will of God. God is not anti-sex. It was God who created men and women to be sexual beings and He did not do that just to torture us. Having a desire for sexual intimacy does not mean that you are some kind of depraved or perverted person.

Second, recognize the feelings for what they actually are. Sexual feelings at this phase of recovery are, to a great extent, a physical symptom of a deep emotional need for intimacy. One thing every healthy person needs is intimate relationships. What must be recognized is that sex and intimacy are not necessarily synonymous. It is very possible to have intimate relationships and never be sexually active and it is possible to have a very lively sexual life and never achieve intimacy.

What you really need is to begin building intimate (non-sexual) relationships, but CAUTION, this generally must be done very slowly. The temptation will be to move too quickly in this area. Quite often those who bond too quickly in prematurely intimate relationships are in for another painful experience.

It is interesting that a much larger percentage of second marriages fail than first marriages. No doubt one of the main reasons for this is that some couples, wanting to get over the hurt as quickly as possible, moved too quickly into a romantic relationship hoping that this would heal the wounds. It doesn't! In fact, it makes them worse. What you don't need at this point is a new marriage! What you do need now is to heal. Don't allow impatience to short-circuit the recovery process. There are other ways of achieving intimacy.

There are other people with whom you can be intimate outside of the context of romance. This will be an excellent opportunity for you to deepen your relationship with each of your children. Even if you're not the custodial parent, hopefully you will have opportunity to do this. Developing a more intimate relationship with your children will not only help you, but it will certainly minister to one of their deepest needs, the need for secure family love.

What about old friends? What about new friends? What about your parents and other extended family? What about former in-laws? Remember, you can't achieve an intimate bonding with very many people. Jesus loved all of His disciples, but He was closest to Peter, James, and John. And of those three, He was closest to John. Jesus was a single, too! He experienced all of the feelings and temptations that you experience. He had all of the needs that you have. Yet, His needs were met in the intimacy of a few, precious relationships.

Third, beware of your vulnerability. As a Christian, early in the recovery process, you need to reaffirm some former commitments. God calls each one of His people to a life of holiness. Sexual activity outside of marriage is not part of the will of God. "It is God's will that you should be holy; that you should avoid sexual immorality; that each of you should learn to control his own body in a way that is holy and honorable, not in passionate lust like the heathen, who do not know God" (I Thessalonians 4:3-5).

Satan knows our areas of greatest vulnerability and plans his attacks likewise. Your greatest danger at this point in your life is not from lack of sexual fulfillment, but from Satanic attack. He knows that exploitation of your sexual appetite can destroy you spiritually, emotionally, and perhaps even physically. When God gives a "thou shalt not..." in scripture, it's not for the purpose of keeping us from being fulfilled. Rather it's for the purpose of protecting us from hazard. When He gives us a "thou shalt..." He's saying, in effect, "here, help yourself to some happiness." God knows us so much better than we know ourselves. He knows what hurts us and what helps us.

Let's face it, it's a vulnerable time for you, so it is a time for you to exercise extreme caution. The time for you to make the decision to stay out of bed with someone is not during the heated passion of sexual foreplay. You need to track your feelings of escalating passion and stop long before the point of "no return." Vigeveno and Claire in their book, *No One Gets Divorced Alone*, remind us of one of D.L. Moody's famous illustrations: "When you're in a rowboat at the crest of Niagara Falls there is no way to avoid going over the rapids. So, don't get yourself in that position in the first place!"

For those of you who are ready to begin dating, there are a number of difficult problems that you are going to have to expect. Some of the complexity of the situation can be overcome simply by making a decision to date only someone who has the same value system as yourself. This is a time in your life when you have enough pressures as it is. To add to all of the other stresses, the strain of developing a relationship with someone who does not share your values of sexuality can only add fuel to the fire.

FOR THE KIDS

For children, sexuality is a powerful issue. They must deal with their parents' new sexual situation in life along with their own sexual development in light of the divorce. As this chapter progresses, you will see that the parents' new lifestyle has the potential of greatly affecting their child's maturation.

She's dating again?

"I can't believe my parents are starting to date other people. They are being so weird about all of it. It's like they never had been on a date before. I hate it when they act this way." These words tumbled out of a teenage boy's mouth. His confusion and frustration with his parents was overwhelming him. At a time in his life when he should be sitting down with Mom and Dad talking about his date to the movies, the roles are reversed. His parents are dating and enjoying it. They are invading teenage territory and it seems so wrong to the boy.

Children, especially younger ones, view their parents as sexless. These adults are Mom and Dad, not lovers. The sudden introduction of a dating life to these children can be traumatic. Television would have you to believe that children find their parent's dating humorous or they feel a special companionship with the parent because they share the common activity of dating. Generally, that is not the case.

Most children will be confused by Mom's new nervousness and excitement over a total stranger. They may perceive that she is preoccupied with these new roles and has less time for them. In any case, parental dating just adds one more stress to the single parent family.

Are you saying that I shouldn't date?

No, I am not saying that at all! When the time is right, you can have godly intimate friendships. But, as the parent, you carry a special responsibility to help your child cope with this new lifestyle.

Coping with dating and your child

Talk honestly with your child.
This child has not seen this behavior in you before and she doesn't know what to expect out of you now. Therefore, it is important to explain to her that you need special friendships with people that dating provides and you have the need to enjoy the company of others. But, assure her that a new person will not take her place in your heart and dating will not change the way you treat her. Then, keep your word.

Be careful that you do not become so preoccupied with your new social life that the children feel ignored. This is new territory and it can cause you to be distracted if you are not careful.

Don't talk extensively with your children about your dates.
As was stated earlier, children think of parents as sexless and you are doing them no favors by detailing your new social life with them. Yet some parents never learn this basic rule.

One mother continually informed her children of the details of her relationships with men and went so far as to compare her new boyfriends with their father. Even after the children were grown, the mother would keep the children posted on her latest flame. Her descriptions of new partners caused the children to lose respect for their mother and drove a wedge between her and the children.

Find someone else with whom you can share these sexual feelings. It is not a good idea to burden the children in this area.

The child's sexuality

Much of the child's perception of themselves as sexual beings is directly linked to their relationships with their parents. Divorced families face difficulties not normally found in two-parent families.

Father's absence

In most single parent families, the children live with their mother. This absence of the father in the home can contribute to serious sexual struggles for some older children. The lack of a father may contribute to promiscuity among girls. One sixteen-year-old girl who lived with her mother was dating a 23-year-old man and had several abortions from other liaisons with older men. Another 13-year-old girl from a split home competed with her best friend to see who could get pregnant first. Among boys, father absence in the home can be a contributing factor to homosexuality. Yet, most problems are not of this magnitude. The loss of the father is evidenced in more subtle ways.

Children without a father at home may miss out on the leadership that Dad can provide when the kids start to date. The daughter does not see her father treat

Mom with respect and love. The son doesn't have Dad to visit with him about appropriate behavior on a date. They miss golden moments of growth that comes from Dad's presence.

Steve and Annie Chapman wrote a beautiful song that describes that situation well. It is titled "Her Daddy's Love":

> *"Daddy, you're the man in your little girl's dreams, you are the one she longs to please. There's a place in her heart that can only be filled with her Daddy's love. But if you don't give her the love she desires, she'll try someone else, but they won't satisfy her...Don't send her away to another man's door. Nobody else can do what you do. She just needs her Daddy's love."*

Hope for the single parent

This song has a tremendous message, but I disagree somewhat with the last line. While it is true that no one can replace "Daddy," someone else can help the single parent family.

Find positive role models of the opposite sex for your children. Go to your church or close friends and seek out someone to be a social and sexual model for your child. Then encourage that relationship any way you can.

Children of divorced and dating parents have some special issues that they must face. But with God's help, the proper information, and special friends, you can help them confidently move toward maturity.

Chapter 5

Leaving Loneliness Behind

There is an old story about a lady who went to her therapist and asked him to split her personality. He asked her why she would want such a thing and her reply startled him. She said, "I'm just so lonely and I really need someone to talk to." Have you ever felt that way? Have you ever felt so lonely that you actually started talking to yourself? Well friend, you may be lonely, but when it comes to talking to yourself, you're not alone.

Loneliness is not a laughing matter. It is one of the most painful problems that many people have to face. It is universal. McCartney and Lennon asked the right question in the 60's when they wrote:

All the lonely people
Where do they all come from?
All the lonely people
Where do they all belong?

Shortly after the death of a very close friend, Alfred Tennyson suffered an extreme case of loneliness.

In his "Break, Break, Break," he meditates on his emotional condition as he sits by the seashore. All around him children are laughing and playing and singing, but the poet thinks, "Oh, for the touch of the vanquished hand, and the sound of a voice that is still."

As with the other stages of divorce recovery, this one is quite painful, yet natural. Oddly enough, healing can come from the pain itself. Seldom does growth occur without some degree of pain. How does one grow through this stage and, more importantly, what should one be growing toward?

One counselor and author says that the goal of this stage is to be comfortable with your "aloneness." Loneliness and aloneness are two different things. It is possible to be lonely in a large crowd of people. Henry Thoreau described our cities as places where thousands of people live lonely lives together. Aloneness, on the other hand, is being comfortable with ourselves during those times that we are alone. It is possible to be lonely in a crowd of people just as it is possible to be happy when you are completely alone. Loneliness is an internal condition which does not have to depend on external circumstances.

So what does the road look like through this stage of recovery? What are the signposts that take us from the present position of loneliness to the destination we want to achieve of comfortable aloneness? The message on the first signpost is DON'T WITHDRAW.

Don't withdraw

This first guideline does not mean that it is inappropriate to get away from other people from time to time. There are times when we all need to be alone. It is typical during this stage to feel a great deal of fear: fear of isolation, fear of the future, fear of decisions, fear of not being loved. Sometimes this fear leads to panic. In our panic we sometimes become guilty of putting so much pressure on our friends that we actually drive them away.

When the signpost says "don't withdraw" it is simply saying "don't retreat." There is a message in the pain of loneliness. Your hurt is telling you to find a place where you belong. Isolating yourself will only intensify your pain. Now is not the time to hide in your apartment and brood over your pitied condition.

Don't wear a mask

Signpost #2 is DON'T WEAR A MASK. This doesn't mean that you have to reveal your innermost feelings to anyone and everyone. It does mean that we need to be in touch enough with our own feelings that we don't have to go around pretending that we are something or somcone we are not. One day in 1808, Dr. James Hamilton of Manchester, England, received a most unusual visitor. Dr. Hamilton was struck by the depressed appearance of this gaunt, sad-faced man. "Are you sick?" asked the doctor. "Yes, doctor, sick of a mortal malady." "What malady?" Hamilton responded. The patient simply said "I am frightened of the terror of the world around me. I am depressed by life. I can find no happiness anywhere, nothing amuses me, and I have nothing to live for. If you can't help me, I shall kill myself." Dr. Hamilton was firm in his reply. "The malady is not mortal. You only need to get out of yourself. You need to laugh; to get some pleasure from life." "But what shall I do?" the man said. He did not expect the answer he got. "Go to the circus tonight to see Grimaldi, the clown. Grimaldi is the funniest man alive. He'll cure you." A spasm of pain crossed the poor man's face as he said: "Doctor, don't jest with me, I am Grimaldi." You may be trying to play the part of Grimaldi: "laughing on the outside, crying on the inside." At least Grimaldi was smart enough to know when he needed help. Men particularly find it easy to hide behind a macho "you can't hurt me" image. The mask only prolongs the pain. Accept yourself for who you really are at this point in your life, a hurting, lonely person.

Invest your love

Signpost #3: INVEST YOUR LOVE. Human beings were created with the unique capacity to give and receive love. When we are not giving love, we are living out of sync with one of our basic purposes in life. The temptation for you at this point may be to say, "First I've got to take care of myself, then I can start worrying about others." What you need to understand is that one of the best ways we can take care of ourselves is by taking care of others. The apostle Paul understood this point very well when he said that the widows who were on the church roll should be involved in a ministry in the service of the church (I Tim. 5:3-16). Reaching outside ourselves to help others is one of the best ways to reach inside ourselves with healing.

We all need to be able to reach out to someone. Ron Lee Davis in his popular book *The Healing Choice*, writes about a young army nurse who, in the aftermath of the Korean War, was caring for the wounded. A war correspondent was watching her as she removed the bandage from the leg of a badly wounded soldier. Caught off guard by the sight of the gaping, oozing wound and the stench of blood and infection, he muttered, "I wouldn't do that for a million dollars." "I wouldn't either," said the nurse. "I do this only for Jesus Christ."

Intrigued, the correspondent continued his conversation with her. He discovered she had lost her husband in an accident a few months earlier. Overburdened by her grief and loneliness, she decided to offer her nursing experience to God. That decision had brought her to this foreign land just a few miles from the front lines. "Once, all I cared about was financial security, a nice car, a nice house. Now I'm surrounded by all this blood, pain and devastation, but I've never been more fulfilled. If I was home right now, I'd be clean and comfortable, but awash in self-pity. Here, my life has meaning."

Rechannel your creative energy

Signpost #4: RECHANNEL YOUR CREATIVITY.
It wasn't very long ago that much of your time was invested in your spouse. Even if this was a negative investment and primarily characterized by arguing and strife, it was still a time and energy investment. Now what do you do with all that time and energy? Of course the best thing you can do is to rechannel it into the lives of other people, as has already been mentioned. But this may also be a good time for you to discover some new things about yourself. It has been noted frequently that some of the world's finest talent has surfaced during periods of great personal stress. Many of the beautiful Psalms were composed at a time in the author's life when he was overburdened with deep emotional pain.

George Matheson was engaged to be married when he learned that soon he would be totally blind. When his fiancee heard the diagnosis, she broke the engagement, declaring that she could not marry a blind man. Matheson was shattered. It was at this time that he picked up his pen and wrote:

> *O Love that wilt not let me go,*
> *I rest my weary soul in Thee;*
> *I give thee back the life I owe,*
> *That in thine ocean's depths its flow*
> *May richer fuller be.*

The last verse of this great Christian hymn is particularly significant. As Matheson confronted his terrible cross of blindness and despair, he wrote:

O Cross that liftest up my head,
I dare not ask to hide from Thee;
I lay in dust life's glory dead,
And from the ground there blossoms red,
Life that shall endless be.

Tragedy can often be the birthplace of great creativity and productivity.

FOR THE KIDS

"It's kinda sad to eat at a table with only two instead of three people. No one yells at me about my manners anymore. I kinda miss it."

This ten-year-old boy's reflections on dinner tell us one important fact about children and loneliness. They suffer the same empty feelings that the parents experience as a result of divorce. In fact, these feelings may be intensified because of the child's emotional immaturity and insecurity.

Daily habits and patterns of living are changed. Instead of having two parents to spend time with, now only one parent is available at a time: weekdays with Mom; every other weekend with Dad; but never together. Father-son outings with the boy scouts become painful, no matter how much Mom tries to compensate.

Often, the mother may be starting a new career and has even less time for the child. The child will probably be coming home to an empty house after school and may not understand what it means to be a "latch-key kid." He is at home, alone, with sets of instructions rather than mother to look after him. New house, new school, new town; these all can be a part of divorce and contribute to the loneliness of a child.

My two-year-old son has a habit of walking into his parents' room in the middle of the night and he always follows the same routine. He walks over to my side of the bed and stands there until I tell him that I love him and that he needs to go back to bed.

Why does he do it? Apparently, my son wakes up in the middle of the night in his dark room and sees shadows on the wall. In this frightening environment, he needs to be assured that Mom and Dad are still there. No matter what the reason, when a parent is not there for the child, loneliness is intensified.

Some years ago, my father was involved in an industrial accident at work and had to have surgery on one of his legs. Although usually active and confident, when he lost even temporary use of one of his legs, he began to worry about losing the other. His fears about his health escalated at an alarming rate. When he had two good legs, why worry? He was complete. When he lost one, he realized how fragile health could be.

Once the family splits up and one parent leaves, children realize that life is not as secure as they once imagined and their loneliness mixes with fear about the certainty of their future. What will I do if Mom leaves me too? What if I am left all alone?

How can I help my children?

Remind them that they still have two parents. Even though the family is not together at the same time, both parents still care and the children will not be abandoned.

Involve the child with other people and organizations that will affirm him. With children, loneliness is tied closely to security and self-esteem. Once the security of the home is broken, many children lose a sense of self-worth. Help your child find groups that affirm him and consistently give him an outlet that he can count on. You and your child can become involved in service to other lonely people. Take dinner to a widow. Start an afternoon out program with other children from divorced families. The world is full of lonely people who are convinced that no one feels as isolated as they do.

AT&T spent $60 million dollars to determine an advertising theme that would attract customers. The result: "Reach out and touch someone." Start your own campaign with your child to serve others and, in the process, put your loneliness behind you.

Teach your child to be comfortable with being alone. The new situation in life may require that he spend more time alone. Affirm your love to him, but encourage activities that allow him to be alone. Reading, crafts, jogging, and other pastimes show children that alone time can be productive. Being alone and being lonely are two completely different situations. Model the difference for your child.

Noted preacher John McArthur tells the story of John Paton, a missionary to the New Hebrides Islands in the 1800s. McArthur tells of the summer that Paton's young wife and baby died. Paton did not have contact with the outside world and could not speak the language of the tribesmen. He had to sleep on the newly dug graves of his wife and child to keep the cannibalistic tribesman from digging them up.

Yet, Paton called this time the "maturing of his faith." Out of his deep loneliness, a powerful ministry was born. He faced the depths of depression and over-came the pain in order to minister to others.

Look for opportunities to minister to and with your child during this difficult period.

Chapter 6

Post-mortem and Requiem

POST-MORTEM

It is important to take a hard, objective look at what went wrong with the relationship. Why did it die? When did it first get sick? What were the symptoms of the illness? Is there anything that could have been done to prevent its death? This is not an easy process to go through, yet it must be done.

A post-mortem of the old relationship must be conducted for two reasons. First, the old relationship must officially be declared dead. A legal document may do away with a certain amount of the past relationship, but it doesn't necessarily take care of everything. There is a great deal of emotional baggage that one carries away from a divorce. Both the subconscious and the self-image are affected. There are a great many questions which, when answered, will help one achieve ultimate recovery.

Second, there is the future. Undoubtedly you must have numerous concerns about your future. Will this happen to me again? How can I avoid making some of the same mistakes?

The ghost of the past must be exorcised. There needs to be some way to lay the defunct marriage to rest. This chapter deals with the autopsy and the funeral.

What was the cause of death?

There are six major reasons for divorce in America today. According to many marriage and family therapists they are as follows: finances, sex, religion, in-laws, recreation, and friends. Someone may ask, "But what about communication, isn't that a problem?" Obviously a communication breakdown is the underlying problem in marital strife. When conflicts in any one of these six major areas surface, communication failures are generally at the root of it all.

Finances
One of the biggest problems in many American families is the problem of finances. Not realizing the hard work and many years that it took their parents to reach financial stability, many young couples want to begin their marriage at the same socioeconomic standard that they enjoyed when they left the home they grew up in. Credit is easy to get and easier to abuse. One author has put it very appropriately when he wrote: "Many couples today need plastic surgery."

But the question for you to wrestle with is: "To what extent did financial mismanagement damage my marriage?" Who did the bookkeeping? Were your spending habits the same? Were you living beyond your means? Did you argue much about money? Were you a two-salary-family and, if so, was there competition over who made the largest salary? What would you do differently if you had the opportunity to do it all over again?

Sex

Another major contributor to divorce is sexual problems. Sex is a powerful dynamic that, contrary to popular opinion, simply does not come naturally. As a counselor, I see many cases of couples who have, for one reason or another, neglected their sexual relationship and, as a result, have taken each other for granted. Were there problems for you in this area? Did you come to marriage with a different set of values than your ex? Did you enter into marriage with unresolved guilt from pre-marital relationships? Were there problems with extra-marital relationships? Did you argue much about sex? Do you feel used or taken advantage of? Did you feel neglected?

Religion

I'm using the word "religion" here to mean church affiliation and more. Having the same church affiliation can be important to a successful marriage. Sharing the same value system and outlook on life is even more important. To what extent did you and your spouse share a similar value system? Did you both belong to the same church? Was it the differences in your spouse's values that attracted you to her/him in the first place? Did you argue much over basic values? Did you feel guilty over compromises you either made or required?

In-laws, recreation, and friends

What about the externals? These items play such an important role in marriage. They can create so much friction in marriage that conflict becomes inevitable. What kind of relationship did you have with your in-laws? Were there times when either you or your former spouse were placed in the position of having to make a choice between spouse or parent? To what extent did they interfere in your marriage? How is your relationship with them now?

Did you and your ex have the same recreational interests? Were you ever jealous over the time spent by your spouse in hobbies or sports that did not involve you? Were you accused of spending too much time in outside interests? Did you argue much about this subject?

What about "couple friends?"

Did you establish friendships that both of you were able to share? Was there jealousy exhibited by either of you over time spent with friends? Did friends ever interfere with your marriage? Did you argue much about friends?

Determining the cause of "death" is helpful for two reasons: it helps to lay to rest the past and points you toward the future. Remember, the hardest thing about this autopsy is to be objective. Determining your fault in the matter may be painful, but this autopsy should prove helpful in the recovery process.

What were my expectations for marriage?

People enter into the marriage covenant with all sorts of ideas and expectations about what marriage should be. You need to try to figure out from where your expectations came. Did you come from a broken home? Did you consider your Dad to be the perfect father and husband? Were your expectations of your spouse rooted in your image of your parent of the opposite sex? So many times a woman will marry a man who reminds her of her father or a man will often marry a woman who reminds him of his mother. This is usually a subconscious thing. Sometimes, out of reaction, a person will marry an individual who is the exact opposite of their parent. In any case, we often enter into marriage with expectations which are a result of our mental images of our parents, negative or positive.

But there are other expectations. An entire generation of us grew up on "Leave it to Beaver" programs and we expect our home somehow should be very much like the Cleavers. Others of us were deeply impressed with the old romantic programs that ended with the lovers walking down the aisle and presumably living happily ever after, madly in love with each other. Still another generation has grown up with sitcoms that portray all kinds of abnormal family situations and the typical husband/wife relationship is absent. None of these models is realistic.

What did you expect your spouse to be like? Were there personality problems in your spouse that you thought would change? In fact, did you marry your spouse thinking that you would change him/her? Were your hopes too high or too low? How prepared were you (or your ex) to accept the realities of everyday life? Who changed and when?

Can you pinpoint particular changes that began to surface either in your partner's personality, your personality, or both? At some point, either you began to fall out of love with your partner or he began to fall out of love with you. What would your former spouse say changed about you? What do you say changed about him/her?

Personality changes occur in all of us as we grow older. It is important to identify whether or not there were personality changes causing your marital conflict or is it possible that you just did not know your partner well enough when you married?

What were his/my weaknesses?

This is a tough one! Our weaknesses are never much fun to think about. What were your former spouse's weaknesses that you overlooked when the two of you got married that became unbearable as time went by? Don't be vindictive. Try to be impartial and fair. This post-mortem exercise is not for the purpose of trying to hurt your ex-mate. In fact, there's really no need for your former spouse to know anything about it. This portion of your recovery is strictly for you.

Why don't you list all of the weaknesses that you now see in your former spouse and then list all of the weakness that you were aware of in him before you were married. Think about how he would make similar lists concerning you. What weakness in you contributed to the friction that surfaced in your marriage?

Remember, this is a painful process, but be as objective as possible.

It might be a good idea to get outside help. A professional counselor or minister can help you sort through some of these matters. A trusted friend might even be in a position to help. If you decide to go to someone for help, just make sure that you explain your objective. You are not looking for ego strokes or trying to collect support for your side. You are looking for recovery, and along with recovery, you are aiming for improvement in your own personality and character.

REQUIEM

There comes a time to bury past hurts and feelings and get on with the future. After the last rites have been given, the "death" has occurred, and the post-mortem has been performed, there needs to be a funeral. Such a traumatic event in your life needs closure. That's why we've gone through the painful experience of the post-mortem. It is time now for the funeral service.

There are some therapists who actually recommend a kind of funeral service in a literal way. Some counselors have their clients write down a funeral oration and then, along with the marriage license or divorce decree, have a burial or cremation service. At first this may sound strange, but think about it! Marriage is the most intimate of relationships. A simple legal document may end it in the eyes of the law, but what about emotionally? I have known formerly married people who have lived all their lives in the constant hope that someday something would happen to get them and their former mate back together. I have known others who have harbored bitterness and guilt for years because they never experienced emotional closure.

The rest of this chapter will provide you with some questions which will help you come to grips with the spiritual aspect of what's going on in your life now. You may want to write the answers down on a sheet of paper and then at a special time burn them and, as the smoke goes up, realize that the former relationship is finished.

It is important to get on with the future. The entire scope of the gospel story was to redeem us from a difficult and sinful past. Paul made it clear in II Corinthians 5:17: "Therefore, if anyone is in Christ, he is a new creation: the old has gone, the new has come!" Abraham looked to the future. It was said of him and his family, "If they had been thinking of the country they had left, they would have had opportunity to return. Instead, they were longing for a better country, a heavenly one. Therefore, God is not ashamed to be called their God, for he has prepared a city for them" (Hebrews 11:14-16). It's time for you to leave the country from which you've come and enter the new land to which God is leading you.

What is God wanting to teach me?

The scriptures are very clear about the fact that God disciplines His children (Heb. 12:6). Does this mean that God wanted the divorce? Absolutely not! God hates divorce (Mal. 2:16). The Bible does not say that all things in the Christian's life are good. But it does say that all things can "work together for good" (Rom. 8:28).

So what good can come out of this dreadful experience? What have you learned about yourself and others? What is God teaching you about life? It is very important that you begin giving your life to God so that He can work His healing in your life. Jesus Christ is called by some the "Great Physician" and the Bible calls him "Wonderful Counselor" (Is. 9:6).

Forgiveness must be a part of your new life. Undoubtedly there are painful events in your past that must be released. To what extent have you forgiven your former spouse and to what extent have you forgiven yourself? It is time to do what is necessary to achieve forgiveness. Even if you are not yet at a point where you can forgive, you must bring yourself to a point where you can empty yourself of bitterness.

What is my relationship with the Lord?

Paul exhorted the Corinthian Christians "Examine yourselves to see whether you are in the faith; test yourselves" (II Cor. 13:5). Satan likes nothing better than to use the trauma of broken relationships to drive people away from the Lord. How is your prayer life? How much are you in the Word? What is your church attendance like? Who are your closest friends?

One of the most dangerous things about broken marriages is that souls are in jeopardy. One of the great things about being a Christian is that, as someone has said, "Christianity is always the land of beginning again." It doesn't matter so much where you have been as it does where you are headed. As has already been stated, if you need to repent, do so. If you need to recommit your life to the Lord, do so. More than anything else, right now, you need a strong relationship with Jesus Christ.

One of the ways to test your relationship with the Lord is to take a close look at your relationships with other people. The apostle John made it clear that it is useless to say that we really love God, whom we cannot see, if we don't love the people around us, whom we see every day (I John 4:19-21). How are you doing with your children? Are you treating them the way they need to be treated? Are you spending the time with them that they need? Are you resisting the temptation to use them as a weapon against your former spouse? What about your former in-laws or your ex-spouse?

You have a great opportunity to rebuild your relationship with God. A new chapter is being written in your life. As you participate in this funeral experience, you need to realize that the purpose for the funeral is to help the living adjust to the new way of life.

What would God have me do now?

Obviously these are very personal questions that only you can answer, and then only with the help of God. Remember, God is not dead. He is not even tired. He still answers prayer.

Perhaps the most important question for you to resolve is, "What does God want me to do?" It's important to pick up the pieces and make a new puzzle. The question is, "What picture shall be on the puzzle?" Maybe God wants you to wait; perhaps He's tempering you for the future. Whatever it is, now is the time for you to exercise your faith. It's a good time for you to build your relationship with God and with the people around you, especially your own family. Quit looking back. Turn your face forward. Your future can be bright indeed!

Chapter 7

What About the Kids?

When Mom and Dad divorce, a child's world changes incredibly. "Family" does not mean the same thing it did before the split and special issues concerning this new family affect the child in unique ways. Let's attempt to deal with some of these special struggles.

Who gets custody of the child?

Little seven-year-old Jennifer sits at the kitchen table and listens to her parents tell her that they are getting a divorce and will not be living together any more. After Mom finishes telling her about the change, the first words out of Jennifer's mouth are: "Who will I live with?"

Generally, the ideal situation for a child of divorce is parents who are willing to take joint responsibility for raising the kids. Children don't need two parents any less after divorce than before. By the same token, divorce does not diminish a parent's responsibility to their children just because they don't live in the same house anymore. Parents who can put aside their differences and jointly raise their children in a positive environment should consider joint custody.

However, many adults are not able to raise their children jointly. Cheryl wants to move back to her parents' hometown to get a new start on life, while Bob plans to stay at his job. This move makes joint custody almost impossible, and certainly horrible for the child. What are the options besides joint responsibility?

Basically, only one other option exists: sole custody. One parent becomes legally responsible for raising the child, while the other may have visitation rights.

Who gets custody?

In spite of the strong move toward men taking a more active role in parenting their children, the mother still gets custody in most cases. Whoever becomes custodial parent should not use this power to punish the ex-mate.

Cheryl follows through on her intentions to move to her parents' hometown to start a new life. Bob would have liked to have been closer to their daughter Jennifer, but does not fight the move. Cheryl is given custody of the young girl and Bob has visitation rights. In spite of their agreement, Cheryl is reluctant to let Jennifer spend her designated weekends with her Dad. Cheryl's resentment over the divorce causes her to continue to battle her husband over visitation.

Try to avoid the visitation battleground, if possible. The children do not need to perceive themselves as pawns in a war that they did not start. In other words, the child benefits the most from parents who can set aside their differences and focus on the task of providing proper parenting to their children.

Disneyland Dad!

The non-custodial parent sometimes falls into a dangerous trap that we can call the "Disneyland Dad." In an attempt to make up for lost time, Dad picks up Johnny for their weekend visit and begins with dinner out, followed by a movie. On Saturday, they go the mall and Dad lets Johnny pick out any toy he wants and then they head for more good times. The weekend is then topped off by a professional football game before they start back to Mom's. Johnny hits the door flushed with excitement over this great time with Dad only to find Mom asking about his homework and telling him to clean his room. Dad comes out the hero and Mom looks like an ogre.

What is Dad to do? He has only a limited amount of time with his child and he wants to make the most of it. Dad wants Johnny to feel good about him! Yet, Dad understands the predicament that these weekends cause at home. What should he do?

First the non-custodial parent should take joint responsibility to discipline the child. Even though he may not have equal time with the child, he should require Johnny to perform chores around the house, just like at home. Both are parents, both share responsibility.

If Dad refuses to be responsible in this area, Mom should not get into a battle over it. Be consistent and apply loving discipline to your child. You may be the primary hope for the direction that your child needs so very badly. Don't complain or fight, just be yourself.

Extended family-grandparents in pain

Mary spoke of the painful separation of her son and daughter-in-law. The couple had been married for nine years and had two boys, ages six and four. Before the divorce, the boys would sleep over at Grandma's house at least once a month. Now, she doesn't even know where the boys are. Their mother had left suddenly after the divorce to start a new life. "I just wish that I could send them something for Christmas," Mary said. Just as when a rock is dropped into a puddle, the circle wave pushes ever outward and the ramifications seem endless. The disturbance in the family affects others who love that family. Among those suffering the greatest blows are the grandparents.

Out of control
The grandparents feel out of control and maybe even manipulated by the divorce process. They are not in decision-making positions and yet their relationships with their children and grandchildren are at stake. A daughter-in-law's anger toward an unloving husband may be transferred to completely innocent grandparents and she may react by not allowing the children to see their Granny and Grandad any more. Yet, even though

these visits may seem too painful to bear at the moment, think about the implications of severing ties with your in-laws after divorce.

Grandparents' rights

The grandparents have a right to see their grandchildren unless they contributed to harming those children. The courts are beginning to recognize their rights. In fact, many states give grandparents the option to set up visitation times with their grandchildren.

Extended help

Grandparents can be very helpful during distressing times, since the children already know and love them. They could provide babysitting and other activities for the children during your adjustment period. But, be careful that you don't abuse this privilege by leaving the kids in their care too often. Remember that they love them, but probably don't want to raise another generation. Keeping close touch with the grandparents can be a great help if you don't expect too much of them.

I fondly remember visiting my Granny and Grandad on weekends in Central Texas. My grandad would take me hunting or fishing while Granny would cook a dinner of fried chicken. However, my dreams of love and pampering would have ended if I had moved in with them and I had seen their shortcomings and infirmities of age. In most cases, grandparents are for loving kids, not rearing them.

Lock the door and don't let anyone in!

"Latchkey children" are a product of divorce and a necessary situation for many single parents. Mother or Dad must work to support the family and, many times, cannot afford adequate day care. The result is that pre-teenage children often come home after school to empty houses without adult supervision.

In one neighborhood, the house of one unattended 13-year-old became the place to gather after school. The early adolescents soon learned where the liquor was kept and the party was on! One night, while the mother was on a date, the teenager threw a wild party that went on until late hours, with games that included swapping sexual partners. When Mom returned, she was appalled to find two 16-year-olds in her bed.

Supervision: the name of the game
All teenagers need adult supervision, and that certainly includes those from divorced families. Consider all of the trauma they have endured. These children do not need to be given opportunity to look for love with the wrong people and in undesirable places.

Alternatives
Unfortunately, no easy answers exist. Some parents have turned to the public library system as surrogate babysitters. The parents simply leave their children at the library after school, until the parents get off work. Needless to say, unless the library has structured activities for the kids, this alternative could be destructive or, in some cases, dangerous.

Look for alternative care that is available. Check out the YMCA, churches, or other family service organizations. Many offer after school programs at nominal prices. Or perhaps, a woman in your church or neighborhood, who does not work outside the home, can be the designated watcher of your children for a few hours a day. If you can't pay her money, reward her with love, honor, and clean her house on a regular basis. She will probably jump at the trade-off.

In summary, parents with children of divorce have some special issues that require extra effort to work out. When you sit down in your easy chair late at night and wonder if raising children by yourself is worth it, remember their love for you and the incredible opportunity that God has given you to help shape these lives. Being a worthy parent takes sacrificial living and the ability to live one day at a time.

Chapter 8

Regaining Stability

Normal to Be Crazy

Someone has accurately said that the period of divorce recovery can best be characterized as a time in which "it is normal to be crazy and it is crazy to be normal." Probably by this time you are so tired of the "craziness" in your life that you are ready to do almost anything to get things back to normal.

Think of the areas of your life that have experienced turbulence. Your entire lifestyle has been turned upside town. Habits have changed. Perhaps you have had to take a second job. Perhaps you have had to move out of the house and leave the kids. Or maybe you have become the sole custodian of the children and no longer have any help with them. There are hundreds of ways in which you find your life changing. Such changes do not come easy. The body pays the price in terms of the psychic energy expended to keep up with the changing pace.

Change has been the name of the game. Many of your relationships have altered. No longer do you do things with "couple friends." You find the invitations from the old set of friends are fewer and fewer and new friends are hard to come by. Your children have experienced so much change in their lives that you can't help but be worried about them. Perhaps their behavior, discipline, grades, and attitudes have been affected. They have changed from being children of a two-parent family to being children of a one-parent family.

Everything has seemed so crazy! But will it ever end? Does the routine ever return? "WILL I EVER BE HAPPY AGAIN?" Fortunately the answer is "yes" if you work at it. After several months in the divorce recovery process, patience begins to wane and optimism sometimes makes a slow turn toward pessimism. So many midnight phone calls come to the counselor during this frustrating time. The subject of these telephone calls and office visits is almost always the same. "Will I ever be stable again?" I always try to reassure them with: "Remember, it's normal to be crazy. It would be crazy to be normal. But this isn't going to last forever."

THE WAY BACK

For many people, when stress turns to distress, one major item in their life is overlooked—the fundamentals. The apostle Paul gave us interesting insight into human fundamentals in I Thessalonians 5:23: "May God himself, the God of peace, sanctify you through and through. May your whole SPIRIT, SOUL and BODY be kept blameless at the coming of our Lord Jesus Christ."

In business, sports, in fact all of life, a major principle is, "When you experience crisis, remember the fundamentals." That is also true with human beings. The fundamentals of a human being are BODY, SOUL, and SPIRIT. These areas must not be taken for granted. The recovery process is greatly enhanced when these facets of life are given Tender Loving Care on a daily basis. Notice here, that the Apostle Paul is praying for our soundness in body (physiologically), in soul (psychologically), and in spirit (spiritually).

The body

Your body is the part of you that is physical. It has to do with your bones, muscles, organs, digestion, and so on. When one part of the fundamental triad (body, soul, and spirit) is suffering, everything else usually ends up with problems as well. The struggles associated with divorce tend to add a great deal of stress to the body. Normal amounts of stress are not necessarily bad and may at times even be considered as healthy growth enhancers. Usually, however, the stress in the divorce dilemma turns into distress. Adding this kind of stress to the body is like adding sand to a gasoline engine. Something is going to break down. When major disruptions begin to occur in sleep, eating, and exercise patterns, the body is going to be negatively affected. When the body is thus affected, there will be a negative transfer to the emotions (soul) and to the spirit. It's time to get off the junk food and back to basic nutrition. It's time to work on regaining healthy sleep patterns. It's also time to make sure that you're getting some kind of exercise every day.

The soul

The word soul comes from the Greek word "psuche." It is from this word that we get our English word "psychology." Many have thought that the soul and the spirit were the same thing, but the Bible teaches that there is a difference (see Hebrews 4:12). The soul is our psychological dimension. It has to do with the way we think and feel. It has to do with our mind. During divorce one's perspective tends to get lost. Feelings and thought patterns often become terribly unbalanced. There may be times of uncontrollable rage, tears, or even laughter. For many there are the endless mind-games: "What did she mean by that?" "What is she going to do next?" Long hours of thinking and rethinking about one short episode or conversation often preoccupy the mental process. Exhausting dreams and nightmares are the language of the subconscious. Sometimes you may awake from sleep even more fatigued than when you went to bed. At times, you may even feel as though you are becoming a stranger to yourself. "I can't believe I have these feelings!" "I can't believe I am saying these things!" "What's happening to me?"

You can tell that stability is being regained when your mind starts settling down. There are things to think about other than the divorce. There are other things to talk about and do. As much as anything, stability is a state of mind.

It is possible to control your thinking. A person can only think one thought at a time. And you make the choice as to which thought you are going to think. You can choose to "think happy." You can choose to "think sad." You can choose to "think angry." The choice is up to you.

The spirit

Our spirit is the part of us that links us to God. It is the dimension of the human being which connects us to the eternal. It has to do with the very purpose for which we were created: a redemptive relationship with God. When we are not connected to God, everything else seems to be out of balance. Someone has said, "We are creatures of eternity and nothing in time can fully satisfy us."

Some divorced people tend to lose hope of ever having a real relationship with God. Some have been made to feel that divorce is the unforgivable sin. It is not! In fact, for many divorced people it has been the excruciating pain of the recovery process which has driven them back to God. Don't misunderstand. God hates divorce. By this time in the process, you, more than most, can understand why. Divorce is certainly not part of God's plan. But on the other hand, it is not the unforgivable sin.

For a person to be completely whole, these three fundamentals of body, soul and spirit need to be in balance. When one is out of balance, generally the other two are affected in some way.

LOOKING AHEAD

Stability begins to be regained when we can start breaking the bondage of a negative past and start looking forward with hope to a better future. The past often holds a kind of magical trance over us. Sometimes it is because we view the past as being so great. Sometimes it is because we view the past as being so awful. Political optimist Hubert Humphrey said this about the nostalgic days of the past, "They were never that good, believe me. The good new days are today, and better days are coming tomorrow. Our greatest songs are still unsung."

If you're thinking, "I'll never be happy again," maybe you need to think again. You can choose the future to be an unhappy one if you want, but it doesn't have to be that way. "Our greatest songs are still unsung."

For the Kids

"When will it quit hurting?" The 15-year-old young man asked me this question through tears and resentment. His parents had divorced over a year ago and he still harbored anger toward his father for leaving the family.

When will it quit hurting? That's a good question. People recover at different rates. Some families seem to cope with the confusion and pain relatively quickly while others struggle with open anger and resentment for years. Perhaps a better question would be, "How do I know that we are getting better?" Are we making progress toward recovery or are we just running in emotional circles with our children?

Getting better

One of the ways to recover from a loss such as divorce is to recognize the signs of healing. This recognition encourages further healing. What are some signs that the family is moving toward more productive lives? Three of these signs are listed below. Although this list is far from complete, perhaps it will be helpful.

Establishing stability

The family who is recovering from the shock of divorce will discover activities that will create memories. Events will affirm the importance of the new family structure. Vacations, special days, or even silly traditions can serve to bond this new family structure and generate a new sense of joy. Any activity can become a family tradition. Sometimes, the stranger the event, the greater the memory. One family has a special winter tradition. On the morning of the first snow, the entire family runs around the yard barefoot in the snow, always led by the father! What a memory, what a bond!

The new memories also serve to replace the pain of lost family. If your family had special holiday traditions that are now impossible to experience, create new traditions. Perhaps Christmas was always spent at the Grandma's house sitting around a huge dinner of turkey and ham. The new family could spend Christmas day giving presents and serving meals at a homeless shelter. As the years pass, your children will look back on these experiences with the warm glow of childhood memories.

Develop a sense of humor again

Under stress, families lose their sense of humor. Everything becomes serious and the least problem is blown out of proportion by people who have forgotten that the world can be a joyful place. Conflict arises over things that would have been ignored or even laughed at in calmer times. One of the signs of stability is the desire to laugh again.

Dolores Curran in her book, *Traits of a Healthy Family*, says that a sense of play helps the family to separate itself from the seriousness of work and the stress of the world. As you already know too well, divorce piles even more stress on the family unit. If you and your children are able to have fun and play together, you are beginning to put behind you the pain that has robbed you of the joy that children bring.

Have a good time and enjoy your children. If the divorce taught you anything, it should have shown you that few things stay the same. Enjoy your kids before they grow up.

Pass on a sense of expectancy about the future

One of my favorite traditions of Old Testament families was their habit of passing a blessing on to the children of the family. The father generally passed his expectations and inheritance on to sons of the family, with special emphasis given to the oldest. In our society, we still pass material inheritance from generation to generation, but many times do not pass on a sense of expectancy.

The value of blessing your children and verbalizing your expectations of a positive future is a vital part of recovery from the devastation of divorce. The parent must hope in the future and pass that hope on to children whose pain is rooted in the past. Children have witnessed the breakup of those most dear to them. They may not be sure that the future holds anything positive for them. Parents should try to encourage the children to believe in themselves again.

Sit down with your children and express to them how much you appreciate and admire them for weathering this storm in their lives. Believe me, the children need this affirmation.

One mother who was rearing her son alone told him every night that she admired him for his determination to survive the split.

Also, let your children know that God has plans for them and you believe that they will do something worthwhile for the Lord and others. Let them know you will be proud of them, no matter where their life leads them.

Encourage your children not to view themselves as emotionally or socially crippled, but paint a picture of an overcomer and an achiever. These children have lived through the most devastating experience that a child can know. They deserve your admiration.

People do not purposefully choose to put themselves and their children through the pain of losing family. But divorce does happen and life moves on in spite of the pain. When you begin to view your children and life with some expectancy and hope, you are regaining stability. You are pressing on, stronger and wiser from the experience.

Afterword

While in the death camp of Auschwitz, psychiatrist Victor Frankl experienced the past-present-future link nostalgia provides. Amid the cold, sickness, emotional desolation, and spiritual poverty of the holocaust, Frankl thought back: 'In my mind I took bus rides, unlocked the front door of my apartment, answered my telephone, switched on the electric lights. Our thoughts often centered on such details, and these memories could move one to tears.' Then one evening a fellow prisoner passed the word to the tired and hungry inmates of a spectacular sunset. Everyone quickly went outside and silently absorbed the colors and shapes of the clouds. Finally, a prisoner broke the silence, `How beautiful the world *could* be!' Such experiences provide continuity in our lives and the courage to go forward. (Robert D. Dale, *To Dream Again*, Nashville, Tennessee: Broadman Press, 1981, pp. 109-110.)

Bibliography

Curran, Dolores, *Traits of A Healthy Family.* New York: Ballantine Books, 1983.

Davis, Ron Lee, *The Healing Choice.* Waco, Texas: Word Books, 1986.

Fisher, Bruce, *Rebuilding When Your Relationship Ends.* San Luis Obispo: Impact Publishers, 1981.

Frankl, Viktor, *The Will To Meaning: Foundation & Applications of Logotherapy.* Chicago: Meridian Books, 1969.

Michael, C.C., "Popular Life," London: Oxford Press, 1912. (See Oxford Dictionary of Christian Churches p. 1025 for autobiographical information)

Minirth, Frank B. & Meier, Paul D., *Happiness Is A Choice.* Grand Rapids: Baker Book House, 1978.

Smoke, Jim, *Living Beyond Divorce.* Eugene, Or: Harvest House Publishers, 1984.

Vigevano, H. S. & Clare, Anne, *No One Gets Divorced Alone.* Ventura, CA.: Regal Books, 1987.